CW01646795

Leisure Walks from Worcester Bridge

A selection of walks suitable for all the family.

by

Worcester Group of the Ramblers Association
Editor: Derek Starkey

First published April 2000

Cover design, all maps and illustrations by Peter King-Turner.

Published by Worcester Group of the Ramblers' Association
ISBN 1 901184 34 X

CONTENTS

TRIBUTE TO JOHN MONRO	2
CONTENTS and INTRODUCTION	4
NOTES FOR GUIDANCE	5
Walk 1 South east bank of the river towards Kempsey	6
Walk 2 South west bank of the river towards Powick	14
Walk 3 North west bank of the river towards Hallow	20
Walk 4 North east bank of the river towards Claines	26
Walk 5 A walk to the Countryside Centre	34
Walk 6 A walk to Elgar's Birthplace at Broadheath	41
Walk 7 A wander around Worcester City.	46
HISTORICAL NOTES	53

INTRODUCTION

This book is a little unusual as it is not the typical book of countryside walks; rather a series of strolls largely in the City of Worcester. It is intended that it will appeal to local families and visitors alike as well as the more specialist walker.

The four main walks each provide at least one option for families with pushchairs and those who are less able. The possibility of returning to the city centre by bus is available on all of the walks.

The book is also intended to encourage people to leave the car at home and take some simple exercise as the walks are considered as easy.

For those who wish to take some exercise yet do not walk regularly can easily start with the two mile options and gradually build up to the longer walks - you will feel better for it.

Another unusual feature of the book is that you do not need a car to get to the start - or finish - of any of the walks. Worcester Bridge is easily reached by bus or train.

We very much hope that you enjoy the walks as much as we have in preparing them.

Notes for your guidance

CAUTION

1.) Several of these walks will not be possible if the Severn is in flood or has recently been in flood.

2.) The riverside path is, in places, very close to - and with a steep slope - down to the river. Take great care especially if walking with children.

3.) Entrances and exits to Pitchcroft are either closed or manned on race days.

4.) For walks 4B, 4C and 4D there is an alternative route that bypasses the racecourse. Unfortunately, as walk 4A is almost totally on Pitchcroft it is not possible on race days.

5.) In the event that you should find that any of the paths obstructed please notify, Public Rights of Way, County Hall, Spetchley Road, Worcester WR5 2NP

BUSES

All these walks offer the opportunity to return to the city centre by bus.
It is important to check availability of buses before you begin your walk.
Please note that on Sundays and Bank Holidays many services are reduced and some do not run at all.
Worcestershire County Council publish area timetable booklets which include all services by all operators within that area. The timetable booklet for Area 3 Worcester and The Malverns will cover all the walks in this book. These timetables, which cost 40p, are available direct from the County Council, local Tourist Information Centres and Libraries.
Information can also be obtained from the County Busline,
telephone 0845 712 5436 Mon - Fri 8.00am to 7.00pm
Sat & Sun 9.00am to 5.00pm and www.worcestershire.gov.uk/transport

For those travelling by bus and arriving at Worcester Bus Station.
Leave the bus station by the downhill exit (sign says to "Riverside and the Butts") Cross a busy road and go forward towards the riverside.
Cross over Croft Road, (another very busy one)
If you are intending to walk No 4, turn right.
Otherwise, turn left and walk the short distance to Worcester Bridge.

Walk 1

Along the South East bank of the Severn to Kempsey

A selection of four walks along the south east bank of the River Severn towards Kempsey. Each walk provides the opportunity to return by bus if required.

Walk 1A	Worcester Bridge - Diglis Lock - Commandery - Glover's Needle. Suitable for push chairs.
Walk 1B	Worcester Bridge - Cherry Orchard via Duck Brook
Walk 1C	Worcester Bridge - Ketch Inn
Walk 1D	Worcester Bridge to Kempsey

Distances	Walk 1A	2 miles	1½ hours
	Walk 1B	4 miles	2½ hours
	Walk 1C	3 miles	2 hours
	Walk 1D	6½ miles	4 hours (return by bus)

Starting from Worcester Bridge walk along South Quay passing on the left the new flats and Brown's Restaurant, formerly a hop warehouse. With the River on your right there are now gardens to your left rising to the spire of the Glover's Needle flanked on either side by the 1960s concrete buildings of the Worcester Technical College. The Glover's Needle is all that remains of the church of St. Andrew.
Continue forward along Kleve Walk, named for Worcester's twin city in Germany, with the old Bishops Palace and the Cathedral high above you on the left. As you walk by the River you will notice the many Worcester swans hopefully waiting to be fed.

Boat trips run from along here in the summer and at the end of Kleve Walk there is a rowboat ferry to Bromwich Parade on the opposite bank which operates weekends and Bank Holidays in the summer months raising money for local charities.
To the left is the Watergate leading to College Green and the Cathedral. In the wall to the right of the gate are tablets recording the flood levels of the River Severn over the years. The highest is November 1770 and the latest January 1998.

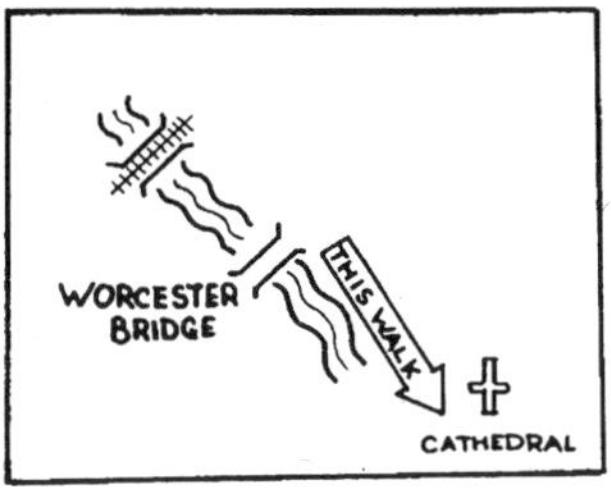
WORCESTER BRIDGE
THIS WALK
CATHEDRAL

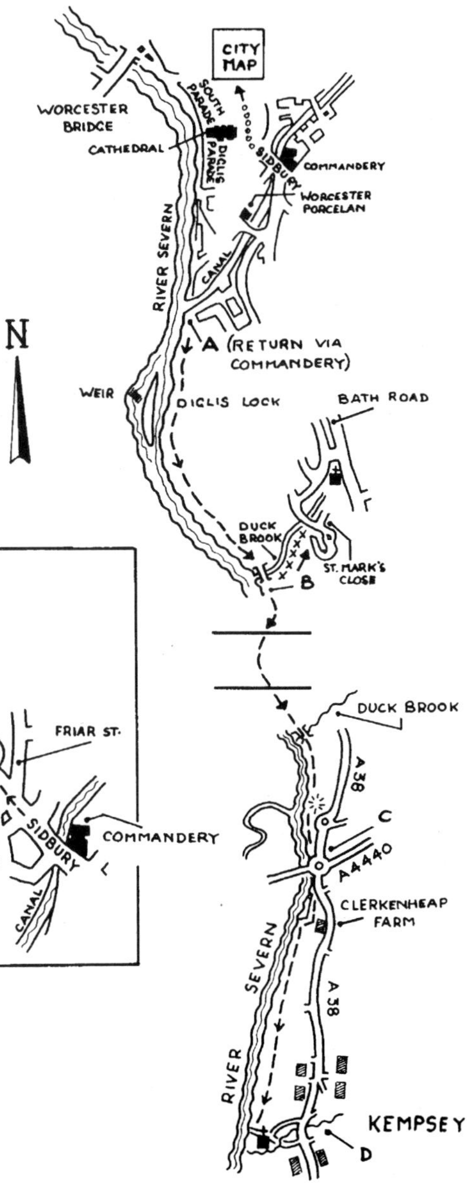
CITY MAP
WORCESTER BRIDGE
SOUTH PARADE
CATHEDRAL
DIGLIS PARADE
SIDBURY
COMMANDERY
WORCESTER PORCELAN
CANAL
RIVER SEVERN
N
A (RETURN VIA COMMANDERY)
WEIR
DIGLIS LOCK
BATH ROAD
DUCK BROOK
B
ST. MARK'S CLOSE
DUCK BROOK
A38
C
A4440
CLERKENHEAP FARM
RIVER SEVERN
A38
KEMPSEY
D

CITY MAP

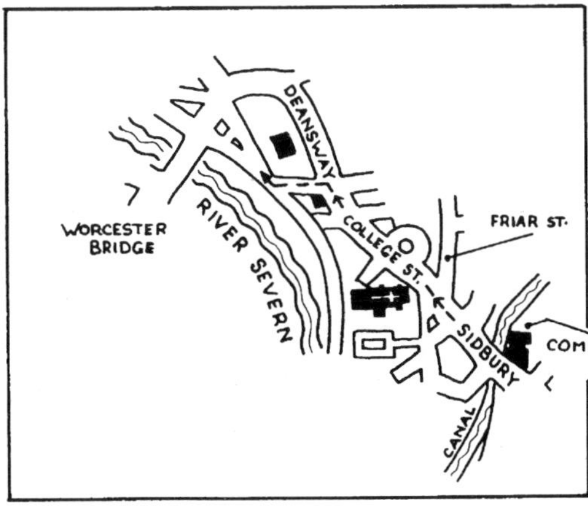
WORCESTER BRIDGE
RIVER SEVERN
DEANSWAY
COLLEGE ST.
FRIAR ST.
SIDBURY
COMMANDERY
CANAL

Just through the gate at the bottom of the right hand wall is the outline of a giant fish caught in the River many years ago. The fish itself can be seen stuffed and mounted in a case in Worcester Museum in Foregate Street.

Continue along the River under the horse chestnut trees with a view of St. John's Church tower to the right. Passing the King's School Boat House a lane on the left leads to the Worcester Porcelain Museum, but you continue forward past the Diglis Hotel with its fine frontage to the River. You now come to Diglis Avenue, a pretty row of houses facing the River.

Over the years these homes have been flooded many times by the River and several owners have raised the floor level of their rooms in an effort to avoid further damage.

Continue along the Riverside path, past TS Fearless, headquarters of Worcester Sea Cadets, until you reach Diglis Lock. Cross over the Lock.

Diglis Lock

WALK 1A Return to Worcester via Diglis Basin, Commandery and Glover's Needle

Turn left and go up the slope to Diglis Top Lock leading to Diglis Basin. Turn right past the Lock Keepers House, noting the castles and roses design on the front door. Take time here to look at the many and varied boats moored in the basin and the resident pair of swans who have lived here for many years. Walk ahead over a swing bridge and then turn left and go forward over another swing bridge past Dovetails Furniture and the buildings of Grist Mill Boatyard before turning left onto the canal towpath. Passing the back garden of the Anchor pub the path turns right.

Continue along the canal, where summer visitors can moor their boats for 48 hours, and passing under bridges 2 and 3, you will arrive at Sidbury Lock and The Commandery.
Charles I used The Commandery as his headquarters during the Battle of Worcester in 1651 and today it is the country's only museum devoted to the story of the English Civil War.

Turning away from the canal and under the archway by the museum turn right into Sidbury and walk past a row of shops, noting the date AD 1420 over traffic lights, and then immediately cross the lights on the left to College Street.
Turn right and follow the road towards the Cathedral. As you walk up College Street you will see Friar Street on your right, this is one of the oldest streets in Worcester.
Follow the road ahead, past the Cathedral on your left, into Deansway, noting the statue of Edward Elgar at the end of the High Street on your right. Walk past the old Bishop's Palace on your left and continue to Copenhagen Street. Turn left here between the College and Glover's Needle and walk down to the Riverside and back to the start of your walk.

To continue the main walk

Carry on along the River bank crossing two small concrete bridges. Pause and look back at the Cathedral and city skyline.
Cross an arched wooden bridge over the entrance to a small boat basin. From the top of the bridge you will get your first glimpse of the Malvern Hills. Turn right at the roadway and continue to Diglis Lock.

On the opposite bank are a pair of Lock Keepers Cottages dated 1844; note the building to their right with trees clipped and trained around its interesting windows. The weir is behind these buildings. Diglis is a mechanised lock, very busy in the summer months with holiday traffic up and down the River.

The path goes on along the River bank between tall plants of Himalayan Balsam with cloud of pink flowers in the summer months followed by the noise of their exploding seed pods. The white trumpets of convolvulus drape the surrounding hedgerows.

Approaching Duck Brook the path seems to wander to the right but you must follow the waymark to the left and ignore all side paths until you reach the wooden footbridge and cross the brook. Those wishing to do walk 1B. should turn left taking the path up to St. Mark's Close and follow the text at 1B.

Walk 1B Return to Worcester from Duck Brook via St Marks Close and Bath Road.

At the top of the path turn left into St. Mark's Close and walk past Andrew Grant's Auctioneers to the junction with Orchard Street.

If you wish to return to the town centre by bus turn right into Orchard Street. Pass St. Mark's Church and then turn right into Stanley Street which brings you to Bath Road. Turn right here to a bus stop about 100 metres on this side of the road. (Check local timetable schedules 32/372/373/374).

If you wish to walk back continue ahead along Waverley Street from the Orchard Street junction, passing a playing field where the Worcester and District Model Engineers have the Diglis Miniature Railway. This operates on the third Sunday of the month between April and October.

Waverley Street continues as Diglis Lane and at the junction with Diglis Dock Road turn left and then right into Basin Road. Follow this round and enter Diglis Basin over a swing bridge. Take time here to look at the many and varied boats moored in the Basin and the resident pair of swans who have lived here for many years. Walk ahead and turn left at the Lock Keeper's House.

Note the castles and roses design on his front door. Continue down the slope from Top Lock to Bottom Lock. Turn right here and retrace your steps along the Riverside to the start of the walk.

To continue the main walk

Turn right and follow the path through the trees back to the River bank, now turn left. The path now runs below steep terraced gardens with summerhouses overlooking the River.

Next comes an oil storage depot hidden under a grassy mound and surrounded by strong security fencing. The path becomes more undulating, passing an old metal footbridge on the left, and then emerges into the caravan park below The Ketch public house.

Walk straight ahead past the caravans whilst admiring the views of the Malvern Hills across the fields on the other side of the River. Temeside Way, including the river bridge, (the southern city bypass) is also now in view ahead; you will hear the noise from here for some time.

1C Return to Worcester from Ketch Inn

If you have planned to do walk 1C and end the walk at The Ketch public house you should turn left into the drive of the caravan park. After a few yards go up some steps to the right leading to "Mike's Way" and continue to emerge by The Ketch public house. Turn left here towards the town centre and walk back into Worcester. Alternatively, there is a bus stop about 200 metres from the roundabout. (Check local timetable schedules 32/372/373/ 374).

Continuing the main walk to Kempsey

Anyone planning to continue to Kempsey may like to take a break at "The Ketch" for refreshments here before returning to the bottom of the caravan park drive and walking ahead under Temeside Way.

Continuing south to Kempsey, there is a choice of routes

1) to follow the riverside path waymarked straight ahead under Temeside Way, which takes you across the front of the Yacht Club.

2) to make a detour which will include the viewpoint.

After 10 metres there is a steep zig-zag path through scrub on the left leading to a viewpoint over part of the area where the battle of Worcester was fought on 3rd September 1651 starting at 3.pm
You can see across the River and fields from Powick to Worcester and on to Red Hill picturing the battle taking place before you.

Leaving the viewpoint walk south through the car park to where a finger post on the right points down the Yacht Club drive. When you reach a metal gate across this drive turn left over a stile and follow the path around the back of a car compound, crossing another stile and emerging into an open field with Clerkenleap Farmhouse away to the left.

Follow the right hand hedge to another stile beside a metal gate. Go over the stile, straight ahead down the track and through a gate into a field near to the river.

The path bears right around the edge of the field and then turns left to join the Riverside path going south towards the tower of Kempsey Church which is now in sight. The path crosses a stile and later a wooden footbridge. Looking across the River to your right you will see the tower and buildings of Stanbrook Abbey at Callow End.

Crossing another wooden footbridge you emerge into a second caravan park followed by the Seaborne Yacht Club. Continue straight on, crossing their slipway, and turn right to follow the path between the caravans and the River to a waymarked stile. The Severn Way now continues along the Riverside but you will turn left into Lanes End. Walking up here you will see "The Severn Trow House", circa 1812, once somewhere for Severn travellers to stay, but now a private house. At the top of Lanes End cross the road and enter the churchyard beside a medieval cross.

The Kempsey church of St. Mary stands on a hill overlooking the River Severn near to the site of a Roman Encampment and a Bishop's Palace where Henry I was held prisoner before the Battle of Evesham. The church developed from an aisleless 12th Century cruciform church into a beautifully decorated gothic church with the tower rebuilt and heightened in the 15th century. The tower boasts a peal of 6 bells which are regularly rung.

The Church should be open every Saturday in August from 2.00 to 4.00 p.m..

Leaving the churchyard by the lychgate walk straight ahead across a footbridge to the left of the ford, and carry on along here to the main road through Kempsey. Turn left and 300 metres along the road there is a bus stop for buses back to Worcester. (Check local timetable schedules 372/373/374).

Those wishing to walk back to Worcester should read on.

To walk back to Worcester from Kempsey cross the main road, turn left and walk about 400 metres to Old Road North. Turn right into here and walk ahead.

There are some fine large houses in the village of Kempsey and several of them are to be seen in this road. When the road bends round to the left you will see a footpath sign pointing straight ahead past the Doctor's Surgery. Go down here where the path becomes very narrow as it passes close to the outbuildings of a private house.

Cross a stile and take a path to the left to another stile into a field; walk straight ahead for 225 metres (247 yds) and then turn left 50° to walk due north to a gate into Brookend Lane. Turn right and after 300 metres turn left into a unmetalled lane (Holdings Lane) Continue along the lane for 0.4 mile. Where the lane bears right there is a stile on the left with a waymark. This points west but you need to continue walking northwards being slightly to the left. Ahead and to the right will be seen Broomhall Farm (a white house). Aim for a stile in Broomhall Lane between a pond on the left and the farm 75 metres to the right. You will be following the line of a Roman Road into the City of Worcester.

Take a path almost opposite to approach a bungalow on the left and on the right a large sign GUARD DOGS LOOSE PLEASE SOUND HORN. As walkers do not usually carry a horn it is suggested that you proceed with caution. Continue past the bungalow through a builders yard across a field to a hedgerow with a gate, stile and small pond on the left. Carry straight on across the last field to a stile onto Taylors Lane. Turn left to A38 and cross the road to the battlefield viewpoint.

Carry on down to the Riverside and retrace your steps to Worcester bridge or follow the A38 past "The Ketch" towards Worcester. There is a bus stop about 200 metres past the next roundabout. (Check local timetable schedules 32/372/373/374)

Walk 2

Along the South West bank of the Severn to Powick

A selection of four walks along the south west bank of the River Severn towards the River Teme at Powick and then on to Rushwick.
A return to Worcester via the Golf Course is possible.
Each walk provides the opportunity to return by bus if required.

Walk 2A	Worcester Bridge - Diglis Weir - Weir Lane - Bromwich Road. Suitable for push chairs.
Walk 2B	Worcester Bridge - Powick via River Teme
Walk 2C	Worcester Bridge - Rushwick.
Walk 2D	Worcester Bridge - returning via Worcester Golf Club

Distances	Walk 2A	3 miles	2 hours
	Walk 2B	5 miles	3 hours
	Walk 2C	5 miles	3 hours (return by bus)
	Walk 2D	6½ miles	4 hours

Starting from Worcester Bridge walk south along the west bank of the river, this is Bromwich Parade. Do not descend the steps but quickly go through a gate and begin your walk along this attractive riverside path.

On the opposite bank of the river you will notice the Technical College and St Andrews Spire (Glovers Needle) Glove Factories were on the site of the car park below the two other buildings of the Technical College. On our right is the practice area belonging to Worcestershire Cricket Club then we pass the boat house for the Worcester College for the Blind. Just beyond the Cathedral we notice the entrance known as Watergate, a passenger ferry operated across the river at this point and occasionally today for special events. We are now approaching Diglis and on the opposite bank is the junction with the Worcester & Birmingham Canal. You cannot miss the large notices warning river users that they are approaching the weir.

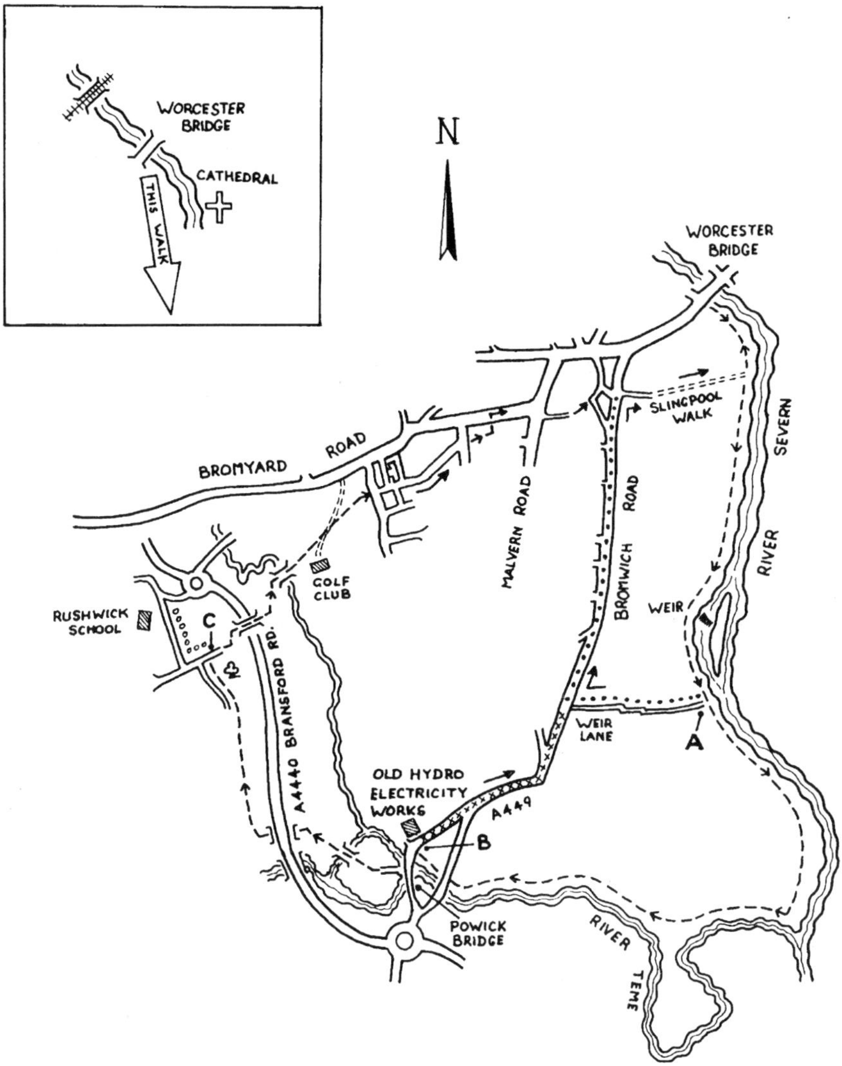
WORCESTER BRIDGE
CATHEDRAL
THIS WALK
N
WORCESTER BRIDGE
SLINGPOOL WALK
BROMYARD ROAD
MALVERN ROAD
BROMWICH ROAD
SEVERN
RIVER
WEIR
WEIR LANE
A
GOLF CLUB
RUSHWICK SCHOOL
C
A4440 BRANSFORD RD.
OLD HYDRO ELECTRICITY WORKS
A449
B
POWICK BRIDGE
RIVER TEME

A large fence on our right surrounds the Worcester Water Treatment Works and on our left is the weir. Soon we pass the end of Diglis Island with the locks out of sight on the other side. At this point we arrive at a path junction and a finger post indicates that we have walked ½mile from Worcester Bridge.

Walk 2A For those with push chairs turn right (signposted to Weir Lane), and continue along this path to reach Weir Lane. Then straight on to the junction with Bromwich Road. Turn right and walk along Bromwich Road until reaching Slingpool Walk. Turn right and continue down Slingpool Walk adjacent to the sports fields of the Kings School and then the rear of Worcestershire County Cricket Club. This path soon brings us back to the banks of the Severn where we turn left to walk the short distance back to the bridge and the end of the walk.

To continue the main walk.

Cross the facing stile and continue on the riverside path signed to Powick Bridge. At the end of the first field cross a stile into a second field, continue with fine views of the Malvern Hills to our right. Cross stile to smaller third field, then quickly go over a stile into a fourth narrow field. In just over 100 yards reach a stone plaque marking the Worcester City boundary.
Next to this is a finger post indicating that our path to Powick Bridge is to the right. Continue alongside the river for a few more steps to reach the confluence of the Teme and Severn.

Now turn right and walk alongside the River Teme to the end of the field. Cross stile (with electric fence alongside) and continue in same direction with the Teme on your left. On reaching the corner do not enter the field enclosed by the river loop but bear right to continue alongside the river again beyond it's loop. Reach a substantial stile at the end of the field at a point where the river swings sharply to the left. Cross the stile then quickly pass through a gateway. In front you will see the chimney of the old Worcester Electricity Works. We are now aiming for the iron and stone bridge slightly left of the electricity works. On reaching the bridge, go under by means of the flood relief arch and continue to the old Powick Bridge. Cross the stile by the gate and go on to the road.

Walk 2B **Return to Worcester from Lower Wick**

If you wish to return to Worcester at this point, turn right and walk along the old road to the junction. Bear left along the main road until reaching the bus stop by the roundabout and filling station. If you wish to walk back to town continue on the road to the right of the filling station (Bromwich Road) and you will soon arrive at the junction with Weir Lane on your right.

Continue along Bromwich Road until reaching Slingpool Walk. Turn right and continue down Slingpool Walk adjacent to the sports fields of the Kings School.

This path soon brings us back to the banks of the Severn where we turn left to walk the short distance back to the bridge and the end of the walk.

To continue the main walk

Turn left across the bridge. At the end of the bridge on the left notice a stone plaque with the following inscription

Powick Bridge River Teme
During the English Civil Wars between the Royalists and the Parliamentarians the first skirmish on the 23 09.1642 and the last major battle on 3/9/1651 took place on and near this historic bridge.
Erected by Powick Parish Council September 1992

Old Powick Bridge

Now retrace your steps a short distance over the first part of the bridge and turn left along a cart track with a notice for Teme Acre Cattery. Pass the entrance to the Cattery, then go over a stile alongside a gate. Continue on this cart track, first between hedges and then as it opens out into a field. Soon cross a concrete bridge over the leat to the Electricity Works. Stay on the cart track as it swings right.

Just before reaching a facing hedge and stream the cart track bends left and soon follows a wooden fence on the right to reach a underpass on the western bypass road. On the other side, turn right and walk to the field corner, then left to follow the hedge/trees on the right.
At the end of this field reach a stile, go over and bear half right across the corner of a field to cross a stile and footbridge. Continuing in same direction go up the small bank into an orchard to reach the protruding fence corner. Then on the same heading walk with the fence on your left to a stile and lane.

Walk 2C ***Return to Worcester by bus from Rushwick***

To visit Rushwick either for refreshment or to return to Worcester by bus, turn left. In 100 yards turn right along Upper Wick Lane to its junction by Rushwick School. The bus stop for Worcester is on the other side of the road opposite Christine Avenue. The Whitehall public house is a further 200 yards along this road.

Continuing the walk turn right. In a short distance the track turns right to become a private drive to the property called Wick Episcopi opposite the Alf Tolley Memorial Cricket Ground. Do not follow the track but continue straight on a narrow hedged path. Over to the left can be seen Kays Warehouse.
Soon arrive at the bypass which we can cross with safety thanks to the provision of the large footbridge.

Over the footbridge we enter the grounds of Worcester Golf and Country Club. Bear left to start crossing the golf course along a track with a hedge on the right and a fence on the left. Cross a footbridge over Laugherne Brook then carefully continue across a fairway to climb a small bank amongst some small trees.

At the top continue across a second fairway to arrive amongst some shrubs, then pass to the left of the 16th hole with views of the clubhouse behind. Aim for a group of trees which include a large oak; notice a wooden waymark by the small tree on the left. Continue in the same direction always aware of golfers. Soon cross over the entrance drive to the club; continue to the green notice board and exit the course on a narrow path by houses. Cross straight over Swinton Lane to continue opposite along Nursery Walk.

Nursery Walk leads into Boughton Street which we follow to the junction with Skinner Road (right) Cross straight over to continue on the footpath opposite (Narrow Walk). This soon bends left to arrive on Bransford Road. Turn right to continue along the pavement to the junction with Malvern Road opposite Barclays Bank and alongside Chevron Motors. Carefully cross Malvern Road, continue along Swanpool Walk opposite. When the road bends left behind the Scout Hut, continue straight on a narrow path with a school on the right. Emerge from this path with Hales Orchard on the right, continue a few more steps then bear right to reach the junction with Bromwich Road. Carefully cross this busy road to continue down Slingpool Walk opposite.

** Continue down Slingpool Walk adjacent to the sports fields of the Kings School. This path soon brings us back to the banks of the Severn where we turn left to walk the short distance back to the bridge and the end of the walk.

Possible alternative route if the supermarket is built in St Johns

At the junction of Boughton Street with School Road turn right and walk along Skinner Road passing Skinner Street on the right, then bear left into Pitmaston Road. Follow this road to the junction with Malvern Road. Carefully cross straight over Malvern Road to Vernon Park Road. Follow this for a short distance to the junction with Foley Road. Turn left and follow this road to a footpath, next to the last house on the right. Walk along this path as it quickly swings left then further on turns right and soon reaches Bromwich Road. Turn left and take advantage of the pedestrian crossing to cross the busy road. Safely over turn left and walk down the road as far as Slingpool Walk and continue at **

Walk 3
Along the North West bank of the Severn to Hallow

A selection of four walks along the north west bank of the River Severn towards the Camp Inn and Hallow. Returns to Worcester via Hallow, Henwick Park and Hallow are possible.
Each walk provides the opportunity to return by bus if required.

Walk 3A	Worcester Bridge - Hallow Church.
Walk 3B	Worcester Bridge - Henwick Park via Hallow Church
Walk 3C	Worcester Bridge - Hallow Heath via Camp Inn
Walk 3D	Worcester Bridge - Henwick Park via Camp Inn

Distances	Walk 3A	3 miles	2 hours
	Walk 3B	5 miles	3 hours
	Walk 3C	4 miles	2½ hours
	Walk 3D	6½ miles	4 hours (return by bus)

The walks start from the western end of Worcester Bridge (St John's end) and proceed along Henwick Parade towards a high railway viaduct. As soon as opportunity allows, distance yourself from the traffic by taking to the riverbank path. Pass under the railway bridge.

Waymark arrows and the 'Severn Way' symbol will be seen from time to time as you continue along the riverside. The Severn Way is a long distance waymarked path from the Severn Estuary to its source in Wales. You will see Worcester Rowing Club's building on the other side of the river, and the back of the racecourse grandstand. As you walk along the riverbank you will see frequent glimpses of the racecourse rails through the splendid avenue of Lime trees.

The second signpost you come to bears the name 'Ferry Steps'. Take the distances displayed with a pinch of salt, you have walked a mile, so far, and it is at least 1¾ miles to Hallow depending on your route.

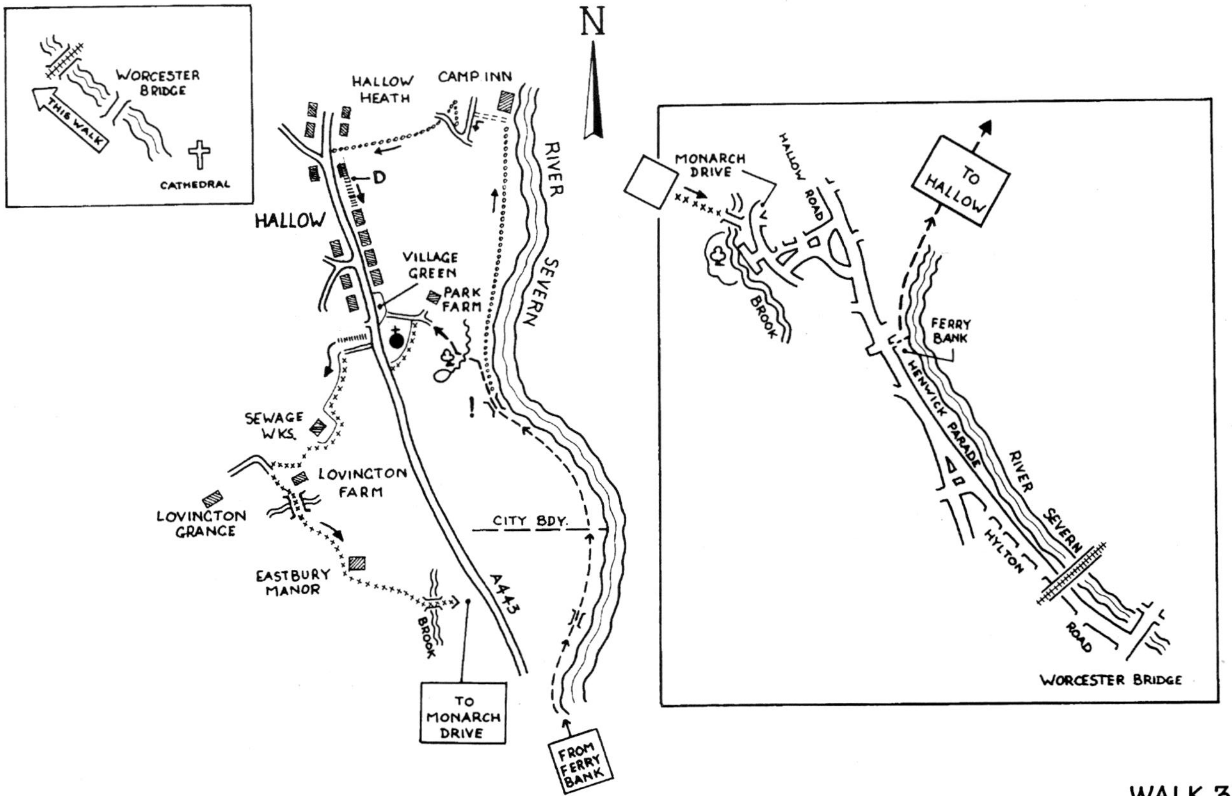
WORCESTER BRIDGE
THIS WALK
CATHEDRAL
N
HALLOW HEATH
CAMP INN
D
HALLOW
VILLAGE GREEN
PARK FARM
RIVER SEVERN
SEWAGE WKS.
LOVINGTON FARM
LOVINGTON GRANGE
CITY BDY.
EASTBURY MANOR
BROOK
A443
TO MONARCH DRIVE
FROM FERRY BANK
MONARCH DRIVE
HALLOW ROAD
TO HALLOW
BROOK
FERRY BANK
HENWICK PARADE
RIVER SEVERN
HYLTON
ROAD
WORCESTER BRIDGE

WALK 3

This was a well known watermen's inn and ferry known as the Dog and Duck, the name taken from the 'sport' involving catching ducks with dogs. It was also a Severnside wharfing, and the ferry was one of the most used in the city well placed to serve the Martley area.

Possible return to Worcester Bridge from Ferry Steps.

The arm pointing away from the river indicates Henwick Road. It is a steep path of 100 yards up the latter. If by chance you need to break off your walk at this point, turn left at the top to walk back along Hylton Road, or bear right for a bus stop 60 yards along or turn left into Martley Road for a more frequent service.

As you continue along the river the path becomes more rural, with fields to your left instead of the houses of Henwick. On the opposite bank the northern suburbs of Worcester can still be seen but trees and, in high summer, banks of Himalayan Balsam, limit your views in places.
Cross a small concrete footbridge, and after a while pass the city boundary stone, where you leave the city limits. After about half a mile you come to a wooden footbridge. **Take care here as the path is close to the river, with a steep drop in several places.**

Walk 3A and 3B Returning to Worcester via bus from Hallow (3 mile walk) or from Henwick Park (5 mile walk)

Leave the river by following a path round to the left. Continue ahead where another path turns off to the right and then when your path veers to the right turn left through a gate to follow the stream round to the right. On your left there should be a deciduous tree plantation. The path climbs through a variety of trees.

At the top, turn left onto an enclosed path just short of some barn conversions but - before you turn - walk on a few yards in front of the barn to enjoy a view over the valley to the northern suburbs of Worcester across the Severn. Return to the enclosed path, at the end of which bear right into Church Lane, Hallow.

For **Walk 3A** (3 mile walk) continue along Church Lane out to the village green and turn right along the latter. Just beyond the end of the green is a bus shelter and the stop for your return to Worcester, facing the 'Crown' public house.

For **Walk 3B** (5 mile walk) turn left after 150 yards through a kissing gate. This enclosed path leads to the church, and you continue forward through the well kept churchyard with its useful seat if it is time for rest. Continue past the large and impressive Victorian Gothic church with its broad spire built 1869. Turn right along the A443

* * * 50 yards along the A443 from the lychegate, cross the road to take a public footpath on the opposite side. TAKE CARE when crossing, you are very close to a bend and traffic coming out of Hallow village can appear suddenly.

The footpath follows a tarmac track, around field corners and downhill to pass a sewage works. Turn right around the latter's fence passing a gateway and so to a tractor bridge. You have now joined a bridleway and waymarks seem to be a mixture of blue (bridleway) and yellow (footpath).

Cross the tractor bridge and go through a new gate then go uphill towards Lovington Farm. Your path opens from the hedge on left to go past a projecting evergreen hedge, then into the corner and turn right along the farm drive. At the next corner turn left onto a footpath with hedge on right and fence on left. Follow this path around corners, downhill to a stream and uphill in the next field.

Hallow Church

The path is well walked and should be evident on the ground. If not, head as you cross this field for an oak tree, pass to the right of it and more trees, your path developing into a broad farm track. Immediately after passing the farm buildings of Eastbury Manor turn left onto another metalled track. Where the metalling turns into Eastbury you maintain direction; go through a fieldgate and your path continues ahead now with hedge on right.

At the bottom of this field turn right over a stile and follow path over the Laugherne Brook, then up some steps into the Henwick Park suburb of Worcester. The path opens onto Monarchs Drive where turn right to find and walk along Monarch Way to its junction with Martley Road.
Carefully cross over to the bus shelter on the far side of Martley Road for buses into the city centre.

Walk 3C and 3D To continue towards Camp House Inn and Hallow Heath.

This section of the walk follows the riverbank, crossing stiles and pass a sign "GGG, Green Park Arboretum" Further on your path passes between a garden and the river, and a sign announces 'Camp House Riverside Inn'. Here the path leaves the river and passes through a caravan site then into the carpark of Camp House. This pleasant old inn is a good spot for refreshments although the pub can be very busy on fine summer weekends.

Leave the inn for the ¾mile walk up to Hallow Heath along the pub drive and, at a T junction, turn left along a paved lane. After 120 yards, and with some fine iron gates visible ahead, turn hard right at a public footpath sign. Follow this enclosed path for about 180 yards and turn left opposite gravel workings at a waymarked double stile. Cross the field, with a fishing pond on your left to a stile almost arched by trees.

Beyond, the path continues uphill near a hedge on the right and you cross a farm track via stiles maintaining the same general direction. Follow the hedge, keeping to it's left and finally a kissing gate out to the A443 at Hallow Heath.

[NOTE there is a telephone box 100 yards right]

Turn left along the A443 and in 60 yards there is a bus stop and shelter almost opposite Moseley Road, for your return to Worcester. This is the end of **Walk 3C.**

Walk 3D Returning to Worcester by bus from Henwick Park.

For an additional 2½ miles and a more frequent bus service back to Worcester from Henwick Park, walk on through the village of Hallow, passing possible refreshment stops at the 'Royal Oak' and the 'Crown'. Go past the pleasant village green and - in 100 yards beyond the entrance to Hallow Tennis Club on right - cross to take a tarmac track right at a public footpath sign.
Now follow the wording at *** in the Walk 3B description, noting that you have approached along the A443 from the opposite direction.

That completes your 5 mile walk.
If however a further 1¼ mile of town walking is acceptable you can turn left into Martley Road (instead of crossing to the bus shelter) and at the T junction, right into Hallow Road. This soon becomes Henwick Road and offers you a straight walk to the Worcester Bridge. To avoid traffic look for Ferry Bank on the left a few yards along Henwick Road. From there a steep path down to Ferry Steps will bring you to the riverside path walked on your outward journey.

The Camp House Inn

Walk 4

Along the North East bank of the Severn to Claines

A selection of four walks along the south east bank of the River Severn towards Claines. Each walk provides the opportunity to return by bus if required.
Please note, that on race days, the path through Pitchcroft is closed .
An alternative route by-passing Pitchcroft is given at the end of the text.
It will not be possible to walk 4A on race days.

Walk 4A	Worcester Bridge and Pitchcroft Suitable for push chairs.
Walk 4B	Worcester Bridge - Gheluvelt Park returning via canal.
Walk 4C	Worcester Bridge - Northwick, returning by bus.
Walk 4D	Worcester Bridge to Claines return by bus.

Distances	Walk 4A	2½ miles	2 hours
	Walk 4B	4½ miles	2½ hours
	Walk 4C	4 miles	2 hours (return by bus)
	Walk 4D	6½ miles	4 hours (return by bus)

From the bridge on east bank of river go north along North Parade quickly passing the Rectifying House. This area, formally known as North Quay, was a busy waterfront served by a railway line. Pass the traffic lights then bear left to continue along the riverside path and moorings for river cruises. The path continues under the railway viaduct and soon reaches the modern Sabrina footbridge. You now have a choice, either continue on the path close to the rivers edge or move away from the river to walk in front of the Grandstand.
At the end of the racecourse buildings return to the treelined riverside path. After a while you will reach some steps and a zig-zag ramp on your right.

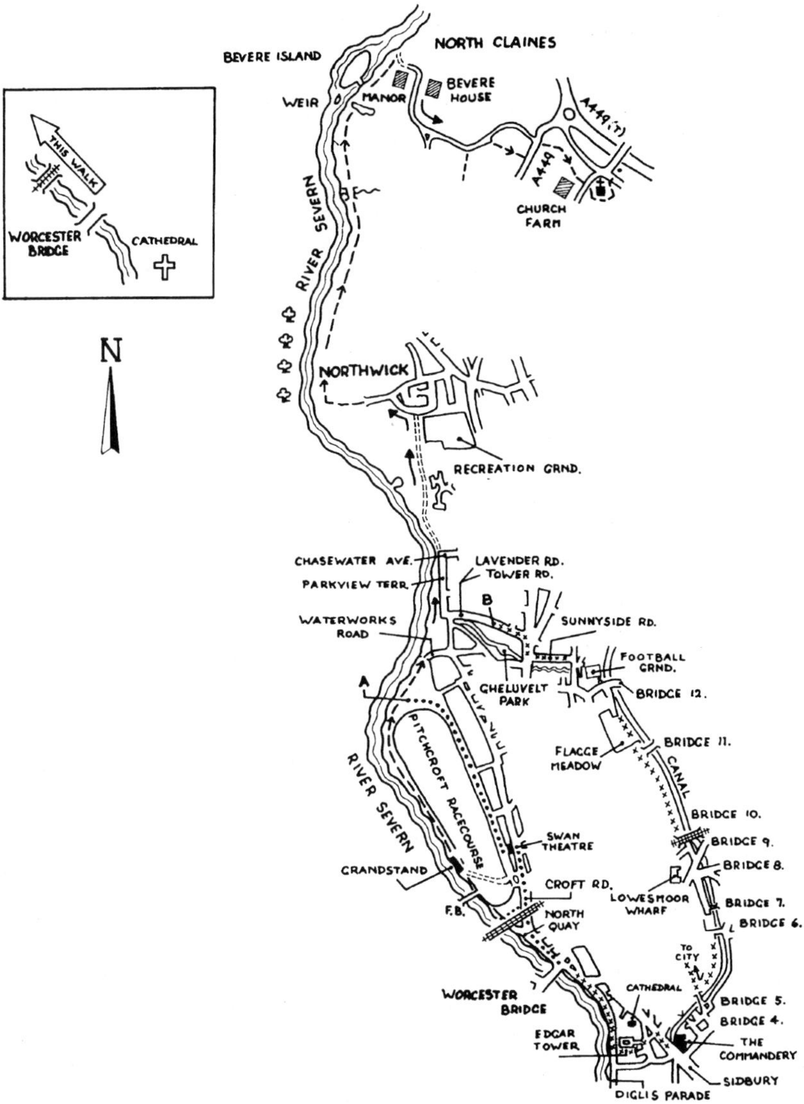
NORTH CLAINES
BEVERE ISLAND
BEVERE HOUSE
WEIR
MANOR
A449(T)
A449
CHURCH FARM
THIS WALK
WORCESTER BRIDGE
CATHEDRAL
N
RIVER SEVERN
NORTHWICK
RECREATION GRND.
CHASEWATER AVE.
LAVENDER RD.
TOWER RD.
PARKVIEW TERR.
B
WATERWORKS ROAD
SUNNYSIDE RD.
FOOTBALL GRND.
GHELUVELT PARK
A
BRIDGE 12.
BRIDGE 11.
FLAGGE MEADOW
CANAL
PITCHCROFT RACECOURSE
RIVER SEVERN
BRIDGE 10.
SWAN THEATRE
BRIDGE 9.
BRIDGE 8.
GRANDSTAND
CROFT RD.
LOWESMOOR WHARF
BRIDGE 7.
F.B.
NORTH QUAY
BRIDGE 6.
TO CITY
WORCESTER BRIDGE
CATHEDRAL
BRIDGE 5.
BRIDGE 4.
EDGAR TOWER
THE COMMANDERY
SIDBURY
DIGLIS PARADE

This takes you away from the riverbank on a slightly higher path on the fringe of the racecourse. At the end of the racecourse the path swings round to the right. Here bear left to a white gate; notice a signpost stating that the river walk continues in ¼mile and the city boundary is ¾mile further on. A on map.

Walk 4A For those with push chairs or requiring the short walk.

Do not pass through the white gate but continue on path as it swings round to the right to continue around the perimeter of the race course. Continue between trees and after some distance reach to car park at the rear of the Swan Theatre.

Continue through the car park and at the end of the houses on the left turn left through the gate then turn right on the road.

Pass the ornamental main entrance gates to Pitchcroft and continue along Croft Road. You may either continue along the pavement to the river bridge or turn right before the viaduct and return by the riverside path to the bridge.

Continuing the main walk to Claines

Now on a road that swings right then passes the old waterworks on the left.

* * * Continue along this road (Waterworks Road) to a point where it turns sharp right. Here turn left along a path with hedge on right, fence on left then turn right to enter Gheluvelt Park alongside Barbourne Brook. Follow the right hand bank of the brook as it curves round to reach a bridge which you cross; note island bandstand to right. Now swing right to make your way to the main entrance of the park and the main road.

Whether it is your intention to walk through the park or on to Claines, you would be well advised to take a close look at the gates and arch entrance to the park.

The park is named after the Belgian village of the same name which is some 5 miles from the town of Ypres. It was on the 31st October 1914 that the 2nd Battalion, The Worcestershire Regiment made their famous attack at Gheluvelt Chateau and drove back the German forces. More details of this charge, with fixed bayonets, and which prevented an enemy breakthrough, are inscribed on plaques adjacent to the gates. Also worth a look is the row of arms houses originally built for veterans of the Great War.

The regimental museum of the Worcestershire Regiment is situated on the upper floors of the Central Library in Foregate Street. It is well worth a visit.

Gheluvelt Park Gates

Walk 4B Return to Worcester from Gheluvelt Park via canal.

From the main entrance carefully cross Barbourne Road close to the junction with Ombersley Road and Droitwich Road. Note the old Toll House in the fork between the roads and the old gatehouse now a bridal gown shop opposite. Bear right to walk back towards the town. In 100 yds turn left into Sunnyside Road. On reaching the junction at the end turn right to continue along St George's Walk. Over to your left notice the site of a former glove factory now Inca Tooling. Continue past Goddard Road on your left and at the next junction turn left into St George's Lane North. Bear left to walk in front of the football ground, quickly arrive at the Cavalier Tavern and the road bridge over the canal.

Go down the steps on your left into the car park and join the canal towpath. Turn right to pass under bridge No 12, continue along this towpath to return to Worcester. Soon pass the sportsfield for Worcester Royal Grammer School Flagge Meadow. Then pass by an older part of Worcester known as the Arboretum which was once the site of the Arboretum Gardens.

The present houses were built in the 1860's. Opposite here are allotments and a high wall retaining Lansdowne Crescent.
By the next tall bridge No 10, which carries the main railway line, leave the canal to walk over the bridge spanning the entrance to Lowesmoor Wharf. Immediately rejoin the towpath to then walk under bridge No 9. Now in a more industrial part of Worcester with remains of the site of Heenan & Froudes, the old city gas works and Hardy & Padmores iron founders.

Pass under bridge No 8. On reaching bridge No 5 you again have to leave the towpath to carefully cross the road. You may return to the city at this point by turning right along the road as signed to City Centre. Turn left over the bridge and immediately right and in a short distance rejoin the towpath now on the opposite bank. We soon reach blockhouse lock and the old lock keepers cottage. Pass under bridge No 4 which carries Lock Street. A little further on we reach the next lock by the Commandary and the Commandary Visitors Centre.

Leave the canal and pass under the arch of the Commandary Gateway (Note that these gates close at sunset). Turn right on road, Sidbury Carefully cross over this busy road bear right to walk up to City Wells House and Edgar Street turn left walk up to and under Edgar Tower (St Marys Gate). Continue across College Green and in the far left hand corner go down the steps and through the watergate. Turn right and continue along the river to reach the bridge.

To continue on the longer walk
Bear left to take the path up to Lavender Road. Turn left, follow Lavender Road, which becomes Tower Road, to a corner and turns right to become Park View Terrace. Continue on this unsurfaced road as you pass the buildings of the 5th Worcester Sea Scout Group and just beyond the house on the left is Kepax Ferry Cottage, one of the several ferry crossing points on the river.
On reaching the junction of Park View Terrace and Chasewater Avenue, continue straight on along a narrow path with a finger post indicating Riverside Path Northwick. At first between wooden fence and brick wall, then a fence on left. Walk past iron posts until you pass the entrance to Westview House.

The path now becomes narrower and eventually emerges at a road where you cross straight over to continue on the narrow path opposite. Now walk alongside Northwick Tennis Club and note the spire of Hallow Church over to your left. You have now reached a playing field; continue along the left hand side towards houses, then on a short paved path between houses to a road, turn left. The road soon swings right and reaches the junction of Constance Road with the unsurfaced Old Northwick Lane; turn left. **# # # If returning by bus from Northwick turn right.**
Continue on this unsurfaced track as it twists and turns to arrive at a field by the river. In the field bear right to find a stile leading onto a riverside path with a wet area to the right. This area is known as the slip. (ancient wharf).

4C # # # Return to Worcester by bus from Northwick

Continue along Old Northwick Lane ignoring all side turns to reach the junction with Northwick Road and your bus stop.
Turn right then left along Beckett Road to reach Ombersley Road and your bus stop.

Continuing main walk.

At the next stile cross over into another field. Continue alongside the river to a substantial footbridge into the next field. On the opposite bank of the river you will notice that the grounds have been landscaped to some extent. Walk No 3 will give you a better view of these grounds. A stile and small ditch crossing bring us into a further field which we again leave by a stile, then pass under an electricity line. On the opposite bank you will notice The Camp Inn.

Cross a stile beneath a Horse Chestnut tree and walk along the outside of a property on your right, then cross another stile into a field with a full view of Bevere Weir and Lock. Cross this field close to the river then cross a stile by the weir and a small stream on right. Pass the old and now unsafe bridge to Bevere Island and level with the end of the island cross a stile. Pass a waymark post then the large notice for river craft informing them of the weir to reach a stile. Cross stile, with numerous notices, then in 10 paces path swings right and climbs away from the river between trees and emerges on the edge of a field with the high wall of a property on the right.

Stay close to the wall on your right to reach a track junction with gate into field on left, bear right to continue between walls to a gate.
Through gate continuing on track quickly passing through second gate and noting finger post to river. Our track now becomes surfaced between lower walls. At a fork in the road bear left and pass the ornamental entrance to Bevere House.
At the top of a short rise the road swings sharp left; ignore footpath sign on right. In a further 100yds, when the road again swings left just past a gas pumping station, find a finger post on your right and climb steps onto a fenced path alongside the pumping station. Cross over stile into field, go forward for 50 yds to crossing track and continue on right hand side of facing hedge. Follow this hedge to reach a corner and find hidden stile in facing hedge.

Over stile onto main road, turn left then carefully cross road opposite bus stop to go through gap in hedge by finger post. Continue to cross field roughly on a line slightly to the right of a house which is also to the right of the church.
At the end of the field go along a short hedged path to reach Cornmeadow Lane and turn left, then right to enter the churchyard and Mug House Inn. Leave the churchyard by the far gate and walk to the cross roads on your left, turn right and walk up School Brow crossing bridge over dual carriageway. Although there is no bus stop buses will stop here if hailed and return you to the city centre.

Avoiding Pitchcroft on race days.
On race days the gate at point A is usually padlocked, so avoid the riverside and stay on Croft Road under the railway viaduct and when main road swings right turn off left (straight on) along The Moors, pass the Swan Theatre, and when the Moors also swings right turn off left (straight on) along a surfaced walk called Stephenson Road. Note the old orchard with mistletoe on the left. Pass Thorneloe on the left, and a fine brand new house on the right at which point the road swings right. Keep straight on along a narrow passage with fields on the left until it comes to an end; then turn right and left into Pope Iron Road. Pass New Pope Iron Inn and at the end of the road turn right into Waterworks Road rejoining the walk at * * *

The Guildhall

Watergate

Walk 5

A walk to the Countryside Centre

A circular walk of approximately 9½ miles.

This walk can conveniently be split into two walks of 5½ and 4 miles respectively. The first walk ends at the London / Whittington road junction by catching a bus back to the city centre. It is also possible to catch a bus from the city centre to this point (Red Hill) to commence the shorter walk at the point marked in the description.

This walk takes in many interesting features of Worcester and visits several open spaces on the route.

From Worcester Bridge walk downstream on the east bank (South Quay) passing the Cathedral; at the ferry steps notice flood levels on wall to your left. You may wish to feed the water birds with bread. Continue passing Diglis Hotel to reach swing bridge across the Worcester to Birmingham Canal where it joins the River Severn; notice signpost on your right 'Birmingham 30 miles and 58 locks'. Cross swing bridge, turn left and follow towpath up two flights of locks. At second flight path bears right to cross a second swing bridge then turn left to cross third swing bridge and go ahead. The canal basin on you right was once a busy industrial area.

Just before reaching road turn left behind Anchor public house to follow canal towpath. Before reaching first bridge note the buildings on your left which were the Albion Flour Mills that loaded grain brought up river, coal brought down from the Black Country and flour taken back by canal barge. These buildings are now part of Royal Worcester Porcelain the back of which is on your left as you pass under the bridge (No2) and again serviced with coal and china clay and china products transported away by canal in years gone by.

WALK 5

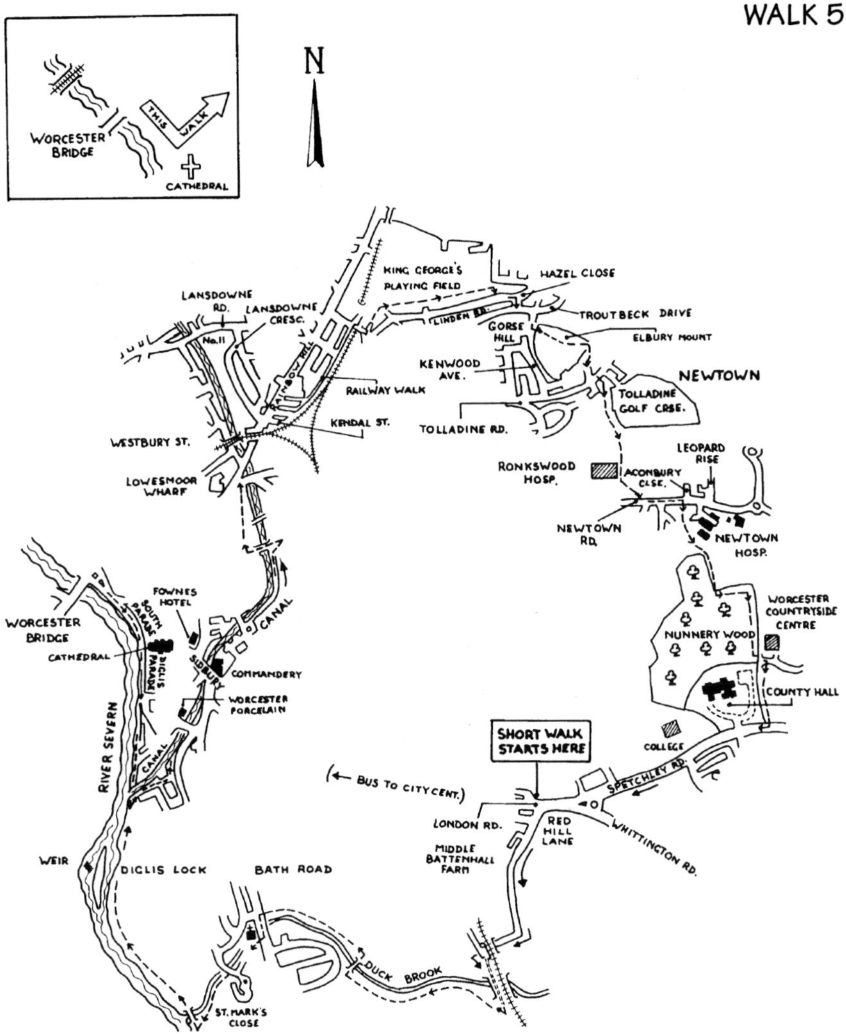

WORCESTER BRIDGE
THIS WALK
CATHEDRAL
N
KING GEORGE'S PLAYING FIELD
HAZEL CLOSE
LANSDOWNE RD.
LANSDOWNE CRESC.
No.11
LINDEN RD.
TROUTBECK DRIVE
GORSE HILL
ELBURY MOUNT
KENWOOD AVE.
NEWTOWN
RAILWAY WALK
TOLLADINE GOLF CRSE.
KENDAL ST.
TOLLADINE RD.
WESTBURY ST.
LEOPARD RISE
RONKSWOOD HOSP.
ACONBURY CLSE.
LOWESMOOR WHARF
NEWTOWN RD.
NEWTOWN HOSP.
FOWNES HOTEL
WORCESTER BRIDGE
SOUTH PARADE
CATHEDRAL
DIGLIS PARADE
CANAL
SIDBURY
COMMANDERY
WORCESTER PORCELAIN
WORCESTER COUNTRYSIDE CENTRE
NUNNERY WOOD
COUNTY HALL
SHORT WALK STARTS HERE
COLLEGE
RIVER SEVERN
CANAL
(← BUS TO CITY CENT.)
SPETCHLEY RD.
LONDON RD.
RED HILL LANE
WHITTINGTON RD.
MIDDLE BATTENHALL FARM
WEIR
DIGLIS LOCK
BATH ROAD
DUCK BROOK
ST. MARK'S CLOSE

After passing under the next bridge (No 3) and Sidbury Lock you arrive at the Civil War Centre, the Commandery which was Sidbury Gate when Worcester was a walled city and the Commandery was just outside the city wall.
From the Commandery continue along the canal towpath away from Sidbury bridge. On the left overshadowed by the Cathedral is The Fownes Hotel. Once this was the Fownes Glove factory exporting gloves all over the world until closure. Continue under a bridge and pass a lock. On the left will be seen the site of Hardy and Padmore's once a leading foundry in the country. (Examples of their work are the street lights on Worcester Bridge and the fountain in Cripplegate Park). Walk on to the next bridge and briefly leave the towpath to carefully cross the bridge. Beware of traffic !

Safely over the bridge continue along the towpath now on the opposite side. After you pass the second bridge (No8), on your right was the site of the former Worcester Gas Works. The towpath joins Westbury Street, crossing the entrance to Lowesmoor Wharf, once a thriving centre for canal trade in Worcester, now restored to industrial units and antiques centre also as a base for holiday barges. Continue along the towpath under the railway arch to the next bridge (No11) where you leave the canal, climbing steps to reach Lansdowne Road.

The Commandery

Turn right on pavement and walk to the next junction on right. Bear right into Lansdowne Crescent and right again to continue along Lansdowne Crescent. Bishop's House was the home of Bishop Gore, who refused to live at Hartlebury Castle and moved to the House (now Loch Ryan Hotel) in Sidbury. When the electric trams arrived he found the noise unbearable and moved to Lansdowne Crescent.

Follow pavement around but pause to admire the view of Worcester, the Cathedral, St Andrew's Spire, St Mary's and many more churches and landmarks. In the distance to right are Abberley Hills, Abberley Clock Tower, Woodbury Hill, Berrow Hill, coming round to the Malverns on the left. Do not ignore the large houses set back on your left. These were the homes of many important people in Worcester such as William Perrins founder of the sauce company and Joseph Wood the builder of the Chateau Impney.

Continue along the pavement to meet Rainbow Hill. Cross straight over with care! Continue along Kendal Street until it turns sharp left and becomes a footpath, this is Railway Walk. As you gently climb another bygone panorama comes into sight that of Shrub Hill Station. Once a busy metropolis of railway engines, carriages and goods wagons now alas sadly gone - but will their day return ?

Continue along this path as it levels out; on your left is a grassed area, one of Worcester's underground water reservoirs and in the distance Perry Wood and Ronkswood. The path goes downhill to meet Tunnel Hill. Turn right uphill to a bend in the road, cross with care and take unmade road between houses No's 39 and 41 Tunnel Hill. In 50 yards, at the rear of the house on left, leave the track by turning left onto King George's Playing Field.

Pause for a rest and admire the view of Fernhill Heath, Hallow, Hindlip Hall and in the distance Wychbold Radio Masts, the Clent Hills beyond. Continue across the playing fields keeping parallel to the hedgerow on your right. Cross a tarmac path and continue in a line along the rear of houses until you reach the corner of the playing field and find a narrow footpath on the right between houses.
On reaching road (Linden Road) turn left along pavement, cross the entrance of Hazel Close and continue to junction with Troutbeck Drive.

Turn left for 70 yards then cross road and take a slabbed path between the houses which rises to Gorse Hill.
At the end of the paved area go through a metal squeeze stile. In a further 20 paces leave the paved path by turning left on a rougher gravel path which soon climbs steeply up between bushes. Go up steps onto a curving tarmac drive and turn right. Walk along as it curves around to a small car parking area with green metal fencing and two high fences either side. Go across the car park and then a tarmac path towards two metal seats. Pause awhile and enjoy the views from this area.
When you are ready to move on cross the grass behind the seats to meet a gravel path and turn right. In about 50 paces a path leaves on the left, first on steps then further steps; a long flight of steps will return you to the drive. This time turn right and follow the drive down until reaching a gate with a squeeze stile on the left. Cross the road to continue on the tarmac path opposite between houses. a short distance to Tolladine Road. Carefully cross this busy road and turn right towards the filling station. Immediately before the filling station car wash, turn left on an enclosed path to a gateway and squeeze through into a field.

On the left is a hedge, the boundary of the golf course. Follow this hedge through the field as it climbs towards Ronkswood Hospital. On reaching buildings and boundary fence bear left. Walk between fences, then on edge of golf course before again walking between fences to reach Newtown Road. On reaching road turn left on pavement.

As soon as the opportunity arises cross the road and continue in the same direction as far as the last house (No 218) on the right to reach the fence of Newton Hospital. Immediately beyond this house turn right across the grass towards a substantial metal fence housing an electricity transformer. Pass to the left and cross the road leading to a car park and then continue on the fenced bridleway across the grass with the car park immediately to the right.

Cross the next entrance road to the car park and continue opposite and almost immediately turn left in front of a substantial wooden fence. Follow the fence on the right soon crossing a pedestrian path and then curves to the right. As you approach the wood turn sharp left. At the next corner a bridleway sign directs you to the right; here there is a step stile leading into the wood.

Cross the step stile and go forward for about 10 paces to meet a path and turn left along it. Now follow this path around the perimeter of the wood.

This is an alternative path to the one on the outside of the fence. Follow this path as it twists and turns, never far from the perimeter fence on the left. Having crossed a second small bridge soon reach a path junction where you turn left and walk to a corner. Here there is an opportunity to leave the wood. To stay in the wood turn right and soon reach a small waymark on the left indicating the Badger Trail. Just beyond the waymark No 12 go left to leave the wood and turn right on the track; in about 200 yards reach the Countryside Centre.

This has toilets, refreshments and interesting exhibits and could provide an excellent lunch stop.

From the Countryside Centre follow raised path with County Hall buildings on your right to reach Spetchley Road. Turn right and continue on pavement to reach traffic island at junction of Spetchley, Whittington and London Roads. After passing traffic islands use pedestrian crossing to cross very busy road and turn right.

Shorter walk starts here.

At next junction, Redhill Lane, turn left and follow tarmac road. When it forks take the left lane with the broken surface, pausing for a good view of the Malvern Hills. The large building on your left is the Worcester College for the Blind and the hill in front is Crookbarrow , locally known as Whittington Tump. Continue along rough road, then swing right to pass Middle Battenhall Farm (no longer a farm) and under a railway bridge to reach footpath/cycleway. Continue straight ahead, signposted Bath Road; follow path passing children's play area to reach T junction.

Turn right and follow path alongside overgrown Duck Brook, bear left to cross bridge (ignore turning off path to your right into school) and continue on path across playing field with brook now on your right to reach Bath Road. (A bus stop is opposite if you wish to return to town.)

Turn left and in 100 yards before next road junction cross road and enter enclosed footpath to the left of Orient Express takeaway and left of driveway. Follow to reach St Marks Close. Cross road, continue on footpath to the right of 2A St Marks Close. At a bend in the tarmac path at the rear of house, bear right on footpath through a wooded area.

Follow footpath to reach a wooden footbridge on your right where you now join the Severn Way (a long distance footpath which follows the Severn from its source to the sea). Cross footbridge and follow path to reach River Severn. The wooded area on your left is known locally as the Withy Beds and probably were osier beds for basket making in years past. The path bears right to join the River Severn. Continue along the path to reach Diglis locks. The path now joins a road for a short while until reaching a white footbridge. As you cross the bridge it may be difficult to visualise that this area was once a busy port with boats discharging petrol and fuel oils into storage tanks and timber unloaded from barges.

Follow riverside path to reach once again the footbridge across the canal. Cross the footbridge and retrace your steps to arrive back at Worcester Bridge.

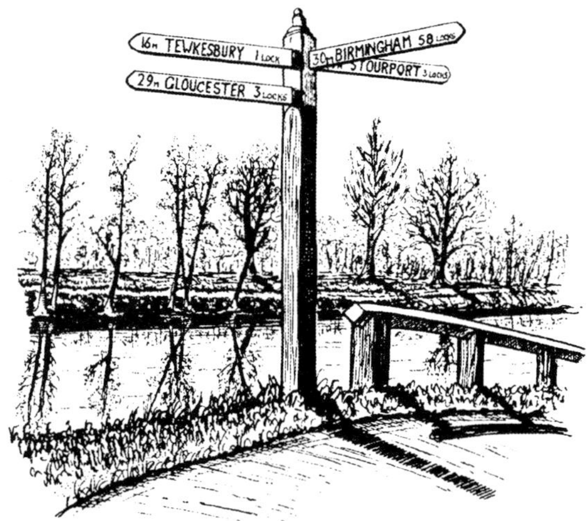

Canal Sign

Walk 6

A Walk To Elgar's Birthplace

This is a circular walk of 7 miles from Worcester Bridge to Sir Edward Elgar's Birthplace at Lower Broadheath.
There is an opportunity to return to Worcester from Dines Green / Oldbury Road by bus, this reduces the walk by about 2 miles.

Leave the Worcester Bridge (western or St Johns end) turning right along Henwick Parade towards a high railway viaduct. As soon as opportunity allows, distance yourself from the traffic by taking to the riverbank path. Pass under the railway bridge.
Waymark arrows and the 'Severn Way' symbol will be seen from time to time as you continue along the riverside.

The second signpost you come to after passing the grid pylon bears the name 'Ferry Steps'. Take the distances displayed with a pinch of salt, you have walked a mile, so far.
This was a well known watermen's inn and ferry known as the Dog and Duck, the name taken from the 'sport' involving catching ducks with dogs. It was also a Severnside wharfing, and the ferry was one of the most used in the city well placed to serve the Martley area.

The arm pointing away from the river indicates Henwick Road.
Continue along the riverbank path for ¾ mile past the Ferry Steps signpost. A long prominent concrete slab will be seen between the path and the river under which a culvert discharges water into the River Severn. Turn left after passing the concrete slab and follow a well used path across a field towards an electricity pylon.

If you reach a large boundary stone with 'City of Worcester' on its north side and a triangular wooden seat around it, you have gone some 80 yards too far along the bank! Turn back and then right across the field towards the electricity pylon.

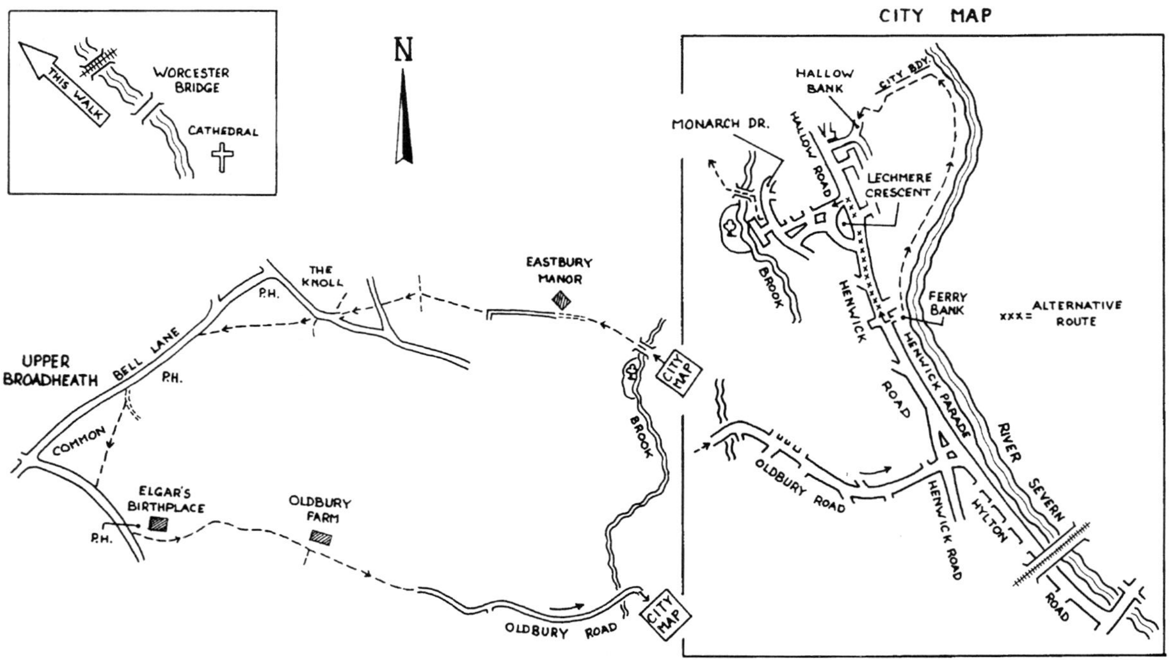
CITY MAP
WORCESTER BRIDGE
CATHEDRAL
THIS WALK
N
MONARCH DR.
HALLOW BANK
CITY BDY.
HALLOW ROAD
LECHMERE CRESCENT
BROOK
HENWICK
FERRY BANK
xxx = ALTERNATIVE ROUTE
HENWICK PARADE
ROAD
RIVER SEVERN
OLDBURY ROAD
HENWICK ROAD
HYLTON
ROAD
CITY MAP
EASTBURY MANOR
THE KNOLL
P.H.
UPPER BROADHEATH
BELL LANE
P.H.
COMMON
ELGAR'S BIRTHPLACE
P.H.
OLDBURY FARM
BROOK
OLDBURY ROAD
CITY MAP

WALK 6

The path passes between the pylon and a long high netting fence (left). It becomes a metalled track, bearing left uphill then right to reach Hallow Road. Cross this busy road with care into Monarch Drive.

Continue along Monarch Drive and look for a slabbed path on the right between houses 34 and 36. Take this path down the steps to cross the bridge over Laugherne Brook.

* * *

Bear right with the brook now on your right between hedges soon reaching a stile which you cross into a field.
Here turn left walk under the power lines and up the field following hedge on left. In top left corner of field go through gate (note blue waymark on left hand post) onto a hedged track with Eastbury Manor on right. Pass by a finger post and then at the entrance to the house the track becomes a surfaced lane. A little further on at the junction of the lane continue straight on, now between hedges; ignore any waymarks on either side.

When the lane swings sharp left leave it by continuing straight on through a gateway to cross field, as waymarked (fingerpost), initially with a hedge on the right. After a while, this cross field grassy track meets a hedge on the left and soon reaches a gate leading onto a lane. Cross straight over (note double fingerpost) and go through gate opposite to continue alongside hedge on left. At the end of this field reach a house and then a gate leading onto a short length of track which leads to the road.

> *Turning right and walking along the road for about 300 yards will bring you to the Post Office opposite the Bell Inn. Here there are three bus stops where infrequent services will return you to Worcester. Ask at Broadheath Stores if you are in doubt.*

On reaching the road note a finger post with three waymarks. DO NOT take the footpath directly opposite but bear right to walk along the road for 20 yards then carefully cross onto a private road 'Knowle Cottage etc and footpath No 25'. This track soon narrows to become a grassy path and arrives at a stile leading into a field. Go forward from the stile to cross the field towards the nearest electricity post. On reaching some trees go to the left of them following them round to pass a gap which leads onto a tarmac road.

Continue around the field at the rear of the houses to almost reach the road; just before the last house turn a short distance on a track to the road by a finger post.

On the road, Bell Lane, turn left soon passing The Dew Drop Inn. In a further 200 yards reach the junction with Sling Lane and Broadheath Common. Leave the road and bear left to take a path across the common. Your direction is indicated by a double bridleway fingerpost and passing to the left of the goal posts which will become visible as you proceed. Soon you will be walking parallel to a road on the left and then reach a road junction.

Turn left and carefully walk along the road for about 250 yards to reach the Plough Inn. Refreshments are available here.
The entrance to the Elgar Birthplace Museum is alongside the Plough Inn. Opening times for the Museum are available from the Worcester Tourist Information Centre. If you are not visiting the Museum continue along Crown East Lane for a further 50 yards, then turn left to follow the signposted bridleway, for your return to Worcester. (The small cottage in which Elgar was born is behind the hedge to your right).

Elgar's Birthplace

The return journey along an old bridleway begins by following a hedge on the left, fence to right. Stay on this pleasant bridleway as it descends slightly before heading towards some trees and then to the left of a house. On reaching facing gates go through onto a short length of tarmac track, the entrance to the house, and continue to the next gate which leads onto a rough track. You continue forward passing to the right of Oldbury Farm house. Good views of the Worcester City and the Cathedral ahead. This rough track eventually merges with the entrance drive to Oldbury Farm.

An opportunity to catch a bus back to the city centre can be found by taking the second turning right, Tudor Way. 300 yards along and on the left is a bus stop. Bus No 33 is a frequent service (weekdays) and every half hour (Sundays).
A little beyond the junction with Comer Gardens is another opportunity to catch a bus back to the City Centre, No 26.

To continue the walk, remain on Oldbury Road for almost a mile to the junction with Henwick Road.
Carefully cross straight over to continue down Holywell Hill to reach Hylton Road. Holy Well was a spring in medieval times and the water was piped to the Cathedral. The lead piping was removed during the siege of Worcester and used in the making of bullets. Carefully cross this road bearing right to rejoin the riverside path which will return you to Worcester Bridge.

Iron Bridge – Bevere Lock

Walk 7

A Wander around Worcester City

A circular walk of approximately 3 miles.

This walk is a brief introduction to some of the older features of the City.
It is not intended to give detailed information about the buildings that are passed on route. Rather to whet the appetite of the walker to return for a longer visit.
It is possible to shorten the walk at various points and return to the start as you are never far from Worcester Bridge.
The walk is suitable for all although great care is required when crossing some of the busy city streets.

From the bridge walk south along the east bank of the river and go along South Parade for a few yards. Immediately turn left into Hood Street. At the junction go straight over and take the path opposite as it swings right to climb up through the St Andrews Gardens. At the top bear left to the base of St Andrews Spire (The Glovers Needle)
On leaving the base of the tower join the road in front of the Police Station, turn left and walk a few yards to cross the road by the crossing at the rear of Beatties Store. Safely across the road bear right and then left into Crowngate shopping centre. Immediately on the right you will see notices about the Crowngate heritage trail.

A few yards further on is Huntingdon Hall. Bear right to pass in front of the hall then continue through the shopping arcade passing British Home stores. The arcade swings left to join the High Street in front of Woolworths and Marks & Spencers.
Turn right and quickly arrive at the Guildhall. Opposite the Guildhall is the Savoy Tailors Guild shop this was once the Golden Lion Inn as will be seen by the Golden Lion high on the frontage. Continue on along High Street and then by the Worcestershire County Council Records Office turn right into Fish Street.

WALK 7

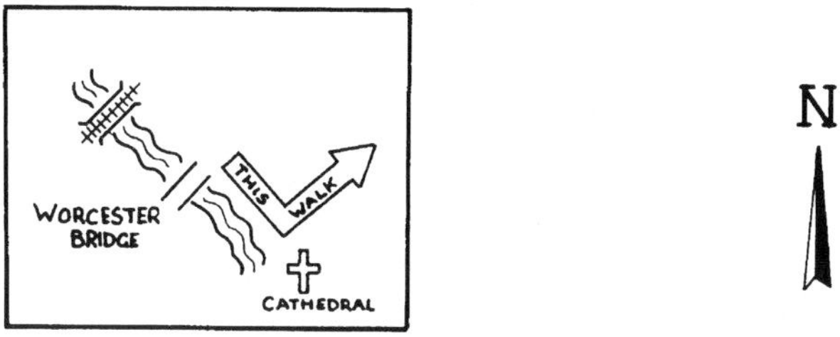
WORCESTER BRIDGE
THIS WALK
CATHEDRAL
N

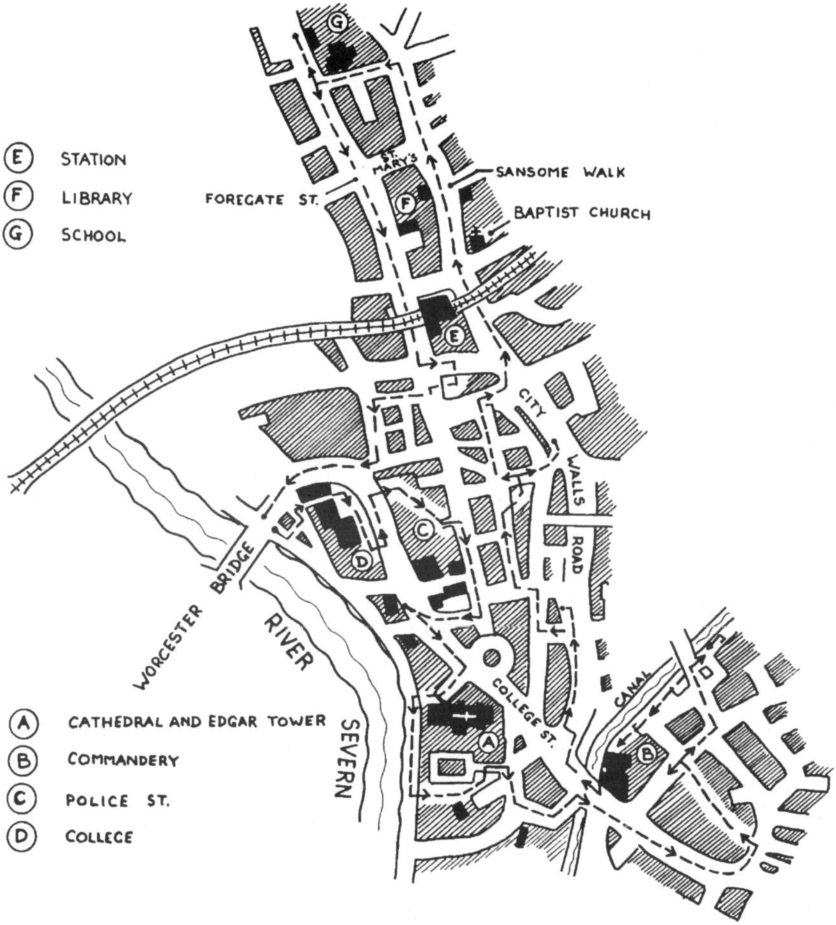
E STATION
F LIBRARY
G SCHOOL
ST. MARY'S
SANSOME WALK
FORECATE ST.
BAPTIST CHURCH
CITY WALLS ROAD
WORCESTER BRIDGE
RIVER SEVERN
COLLEGE ST.
CANAL
A CATHEDRAL AND EDGAR TOWER
B COMMANDERY
C POLICE ST.
D COLLECE

The Records Office was originally St Helens Church. Pass the black and white Farriers Arms. Carefully cross over Deansway to take a look at what is now Maggs Day Centre, formally the 11century St Alban's Church.

Return to Deansway, turn right and walk alongside the rear of Worcester Technical College towards the Cathedral and then pause to look through the iron gateway of The Old Palace (Bishops Palace) If you enter the car park and look to your left you will see the old stable block. Continue along Deansway to the roundabout and traffic lights, note the statue of Sir Edward Elgar to your left.

Turn right into the grounds of the Cathedral College Yard with the fine old buildings adjacent to the Cathedral. At the entrance to the Cathedral bear right towards the west end. Go down steps opposite the west door bear left along the terrace overlooking the river. Continue down two further flights of steps to a lower terrace then bear left to arrive at a gate into the end of College Green..

A short detour down the steps opposite will bring you to Watergate where you will notice the markings for the flood levels. Now return and walk up the slope to College Green; most of the surrounding buildings form part of Worcester Kings School. Walk to the left around the green and leave by the Edgar Tower, into Edgar Street; notice the fine old gates. Pause and admire the fine old buildings here and the Kings School 'Tuck Shop' on the right hand side.

It is worth making a detour along the Georgian College Precincts on your left before returning to this spot. Roughly in the position of what is now Barclays Bank was the site of the old Lychegate.

Back by the Edgar Tower turn right into Severn Street, noting Castle Place on the right, now an entrance to the Kings School. In front and to your left is the Royal Worcester Porcelain factory and Dyson Perrins museum, formally St Peters School. Turn left into King Street, (as you walk along the street you can see up to Fort Royal Park) and follow it as it swings left to reach Sidbury This once narrow street was one of the bottlenecks of the A38 in summer months.
Carefully cross over this busy road and turn right passing the Commandary to the left. This is worthy of a return visit.

Continue straight ahead crossing Wylds Lane then up the hill to Fort Royal Hill. Turn left here and then left into Fort Royal Gardens. From here Charles II watched the battle of Worcester taking place on the river plain to the left as far as Powick. Continue down through the park to Wylds Lane. Turn left then right to retrace your steps past the Commandary.

(Alternatively, turn right, then left at the cross roads into Park Street. Walk along as far as the canal bridge. On the right of the bridge are steps leading to the tow path. On the tow path turn left under the bridge and walk along to rejoin Sidbury by the Commandary. Turn right.)

The Edgar Tower

Our journey takes us to the junction with City Walls Road and traffic lights. Carefully cross over the three carriageways and turn right on the opposite side. Soon pass Fownes Hotel which was once Fownes Glove factory.

To view a section of the City Wall cross over Union Street and go down steps. Retrace you steps and turn right into Union Street to pass Lasletts Almshouses and reach the junction with Friar Street. Detour a few yards to the left to take a glance at the Museum of Local Life, Tudor House.

Friar Street and New Street are fine examples of old Worcester.

Then turn right walking along Friar street passing fine old buildings note the display panel of wattle and daub construction on the building of Ruby Tuesday.

On the right is Greyfriars, now under the control of the National Trust well worth a longer visit when time allows.

Continue to the Eagle Vaults and notice the fine tiled front then turn left into Pump Street formally Needle St. Then turn right into the Shambles In 100 yds, and immediately after the Market Hall on your right, turn right into Market Passage. At the end of the passage return to New Street; now note the fine black and white house opposite, Nash's House. Turn left soon to notice on your right The Pheasant, at one time there was a bowling green at the rear. It was also used for cockfighting.

Greyfriars – Friar Street

The Swan with Two Nicks is a little further on and then you reach King Charles House. A little further on is the Cornmarket. Among other uses it housed the stocks and pillory; public whippings took place here. Round to the right on City Walls Road is St Martins Gate; older residents know it as Clapgate.

In the Cornmarket bear left to walk up Mealcheapen Street. In front is the now redundant St Swithins Church; walk along the left hand side to the main entrance to the Glasshouse restaurant above which is a sign "this school was founded and endowed by Queen Elizabeth in the third year of her reign and rebuilt in 1735".

Retrace your steps to the end of the Shambles, (street of butchers in days gone by. Some had their own slaughter house which were in use until after the war). On the corner is H Samuel, once the site of an iron monger with a forge at the rear. Turn left to cross over into Trinity street. On our right is Queen Elizabeth House.

Return to Trinity Street and turn right; notice to the left Bushwhackers Night-club originally Church House. Continue to the junction with St Nicholas Street and turn right. In front you will notice the County Furnishing store; this and the buildings behind are all part of the one time Hill Evans vinegar works, the largest of its kind in the world. You now need to cross diagonally over the road. This is best achieved by crossing over City Walls road then turning left to arrive at the far side of Sansome Street.

The first building is St Georges Catholic Church. Continuing along this right hand pavement you will see over to the left Friends Meeting House; pause to look into their lovely garden. Continue along Sansome Walk passing under the railway bridge.

Soon pass Sansome Walk Baptist Church and opposite is the dilapidated Victoria Institute. On the right, on the corner of Arboretum Road is The Lodge, the entrance to the 19th century Arboretum Gardens. At the junction with Northfield Street is the old St Marys Church now converted to distinctive apartments.

On reaching a car layby which is at the rear of swimming baths this was formally 'Parks Baths' public baths. Here cross the road and then turn left into St Oswalds Road. On your right is the Foresters Arms at the rear of which was a boxing ring.

In St Oswalds Road on the right we will see St Oswalds Almshouses; a detour to the right is worthwhile to see the front of St Oswalds Hospital and the Alice Ottley School formerly Britannia House.
From St Oswalds Road turn left and continue past Kays to the traffic lights at the top of St Mary's Street. Continue into Foregate St soon to pass the magnificent Shirehall. Next is the City Museum and Library.

Now pass under the railway bridge by Foregate Street station, pass the Star Hotel on right to traffic lights. Here turn left into Sansome Street and in a few yards look up to your left to see the hop pickers terra cotta pediment decoration. Now carefully cross over, and turn right through the arch into Hopmarket Yard and immediately right again to return to The Foregate opposite the iron entrance gates to the Berkeley Almshouses. In the Hopmarket hops were bought and sold not so many years ago, it was also an hotel.

Turn right into Angel St pass an old inn now named The Cricketer formally The Shakespeare next to which is the Kwik Safe supermarket. This was the site of the Theatre Royal which was demolished in the 60's and this concrete building was built as a car show room. Opposite is the Corn Exchange; now a restaurant. At the cross roads over to the right is Tramps night club formally the Congregational Church.

Turn left into Angel Place; at the junction turn right and continue down Broad Street. At the end of the pedestrian area on the left is All Saints Church; this area was once known as The Well. Carefully cross over these busy roads and continue down Bridge Street to Worcester Bridge and the end of your journey.

Historical Notes

River Severn. The name comes from the legendary figure of Sabrina, a princess who was put to death by drowning in the river in the Dark Ages. The river was once known as 'The Kings High Stream of Severn' allowing free passage to all vessels. Worcester was a major inland port and the prosperity of the city was linked to the river until the coming of the railway. The Industrial Revolution was responsible for arguably the busiest period of commercial traffic on the river. Components for steam engines and locomotives will have passed through Worcester.

Worcester Bridge . From early days a wooden bridge spanned the river near to the bottom of Dolday. In 1373 funds were raised to build a stone bridge which became the main crossing to Wales between Gloucester and Bridgenorth. It was an impressive structure with a gatehouse in the centre. In 1764 an Act of Parliament gave leave to build a new bridge with a toll house. John Gwynne's bridge was opened in 1781 at a cost of £30,000 which included the quays. This bridge was replaced by the present bridge in 1932

St Andrews Gardens were open on the 5 June 1953 by the mayor of Worcester to commemorate the coronation of Queen Elizabeth II. Formally the site of St Andrew's Church and churchyard which were conveyed as a gift to the corporation by the Bishop of Worcester in 1947 The church, which it is believed was first built in the 12 century, was demolished due to its dilapidated condition and the tower and spire only now remain. The tower built in the 15 century and the spire rebuilt in 1751 together rise to a height of 245½ feet and form one of Worcester most beautiful and well known landmarks The spire is locally referred to as the Glovers Needle due no doubt to its shape and Worcesters' association to the glove making industry.

Huntingdon Hall. Lady Huntington's followers came to Worcester in 1767. This is the second church built in the area because the congregation increased. It was opened in 1804 to hold 1000 people and was enlarged in 1815 to hold 1500.

"The church finally closed in 1976. The Civic Society was determined the chapel should not be demolished and after the formation of the City of Worcester Building Preservation Trust and many years of hard work the church was reopened as a concert hall in 1987".

The information in this last paragraph is from Huntington Hall, Chapel to Concert Hall by Joan M Knowles.

The Guildhall. The present building was started in 1721 and completed in 1723 at a cost of £3,730. The wings were added later. The entablature of arms on the top of the building is by Thomas White. The statues in the niches are of Charles I, Charles II and Queen Anne. The man with his ears pinned over the doorway is supposed to be Oliver Cromwell.

St Helen's Church. This is the most ancient church in the city, dating back to 680 and possibly built on the site of a Roman Temple. St Helens closed as a church after 1950 and later became the County Records Office. Their most treasured possession is William Shakespeares Marriage Bond.

The Old Palace, Deansway. Until 1842 one of the official residencesof the Bishop of Worcester. He also had Hartlebury Castle and a London house. Now just Hartlebury Castle. In the 20th century the Old Palace became a Church Club House and Diocesan Offices.

The Cathedral. In the 1060's St Wulstan started to build a cathedral where St Oswald had previously built one. Very little of St Wulstan's cathedral remains today. There are two important Royal tombs; King John of Magna Carta fame and Prince Arthur, elder bother of King Henry VIII.

The Water Gate. Built in 1378 for the convenience of boatman and part of the cities defences.

The Lich (Lych) Gate. Dated from the early 16th Century and was the old entrance to the cathedral cemetery. This was demolished, along with other buildings around it, to make way for a 1960's development.

Edgar Tower. Built by order of King John after a previous gate was destroyed by fire in 1202. Known as St Mary's Gate until late 19th century it then became known as the Edgar Tower because a statue of King Edgar was in one of the niches for several centuries. Parts of the massive wooden gates are from King John's time.

The Commandery. Originally built in the 11th century, it catered for wayfarers who arrived after the city gates closed at night. It was King Charles II headquarters at the Battle of Worcester in 1651 and is now a museum of the English Civil War.

Fownes Hotel was a former glove factory. There was a Glovers Guild in Worcester in 1497. Gloving was a very important industry until the early 20th century.

Greyfriars is one of the finest half timbered buildings in the city. It was only part of the Friary that covered land occupied by the present building and Laslett's Hospital. After the Disolution in 1539 Grefriars was bought from the Crown by the Municipal corporation of Worcester. Over the centuries it has been put to various uses, with the Corporation using it as a prison in the late 18th century. In about 1870 it was converted into four shops. Over the years the building became dilapidated until the 1940 -1950's when it was purchased by W J Thompson and restored by J Matley Moore. This is now a National Trust property with very limited opening hours.

Tudor House, now the Museum of Local Life. For many years it was the Cross Keys Inn. At the beginning of the 20th century it was a Coffee House and in the 1920's became the local Education Office.

Laslett's Almshouses. William Laslett bought the city gaol in Friar Street in 1867 and converted the cells to accommodate old married couples.

Nash's House dates from the 16th century. At the start of the Civil War the house was occupied by John Nash who was a Roundhead Captain of Horse. It seems that during the Royalist occupation of the city Nash fled and Dud Dudley, a Colonel in the King's service moved into the house. In later yeras the Nash family returned to the house.

King Charles' House was originally the Berkeley mansion. In 1651 the house was let to a Mr Durant who was host to Charles II when he had his headquarters here. After his defeat at the Battle of Worcester Charles escaped from the city by way of the back door of this house.

St Swithin's Church. Built in 1736, this Hogarthian church has box pews, a three decker pulpit and the Mayor's chair with wrought iron Civic Sword rest. This church is no longer used for services. Tucked away behind the church is the old Queen Elizabeth Grammer School which was used until 1870.

Queen Elizabeth's House. When the Queen came to Worcester in 1575 she is supposed to have ascended to the gallery to watch a pageant and address the people. In the 1890's it was moved 30ft on a greased metal railway to make way for road widening.

St George's Roman Catholic Church was built in 1829 on the site of an earlier church. The architect was Henry Rowe, the builder of the Shirehall.

Friends Meeting House. The little graveyard here was laid out in 1701.

The Arboretum Gardens were 25 acres of public gardens, cricket ground, bowling green and archery butts which opened in 1859. These were run by the Pleasure Grounds Company. After a Horticultural Show in 1863 the company went into liquidation and the ground was sold mainly for the building of workmens houses.

St Oswald's Hospital. There was a chapel to St Oswald here in 1539. Almshouses were erected in 1681 but these were replaced by the present buildings in 1873.

Britannia House. The old mansion of the Somers family, this was the work of Thomas White, the local architect and sculptor who carved some of the figures on the Guildhall. He carved the statue of Britannia on the front of this house. In the 1860's it became a boys school, but in 1883 changed to the Worcester High School for Girls. It is now the Alice Ottley School for Girls.

The Shire Hall was completed in 1838 at a cost of £32,000. It had been necessary to build this as the Guildhall was not large enough to deal with County Courts and Assizes at the same time.

The Star Hotel was originally the Star and Garter 19th century coaching inn.

The Hop Market. In 1731 the hop market was established in the Parish Workhouse building and by the end of the century was the biggest hop market in the Kingdom. The present Hop Market and Hotel was built in 1900.

Berkeley Hospital. Founded by Robert Berkely of Spetchly. He left £2,000 in his will of 1692 to build and maintain a Hospital for 12 poor men and 1 poor woman. The building was completed in 1710.

The Corn Exchange opened in 1848. Since corn ceased to be sold there it has been used for many purposes including political meetings, a boxing hall and an auction room. It is now a restaurant.

Powick Power Station Worcester was the first municipality in Britain to build and operate its own hydroelectric power station. With an output of 400kw it was by far the biggest built in the 19th century for public supply.

THANKS

Thanks are due to so many people without whose contributions this book would not have been possible. Members of Worcester Group have developed John Monro's original idea and revised his text for the walks, while others have spent hours checking the descriptions and making valuable comments and suggestions. Special thanks are due to the small publication committee whose drive and determination have seen this book through to fruition, and to Derek Starkey for co-ordinating the project.

We are very grateful to local historian Bill Gwilliam who has very generously allowed us to make reference to his book "Old Worcester: People and Places".

Thanks are also due to Peter King-Turner for producing the maps and illustrations.

Old Hydro Electric Works